INSIDE THE
NFL

D1449143

CLEVELAND
BROWNS

BY TONY HUNTER

SportsZone

An Imprint of Abdo Publishing
abdobooks.com

abdobooks.com

Published by Abdo Publishing, a division of ABDO, PO Box 398166, Minneapolis, Minnesota 55439. Copyright © 2020 by Abdo Consulting Group, Inc. International copyrights reserved in all countries. No part of this book may be reproduced in any form without written permission from the publisher. SportsZone™ is a trademark and logo of Abdo Publishing.

Printed in the United States of America, North Mankato, Minnesota
022019
092019

Cover Photo ©: Rick Osentoski/AP Images
Interior Photos ©: Ferd Kaufman/AP Images, 4; NFL Photos/AP Images, 7, 25, 27; AP Images, 9, 11, 12, 18, 43; Pro Football Hall of Fame/AP Images, 15; Neil Leifer/Sports Illustrated/Getty Images, 21; Heinz Kluetmeier/Sports Illustrated/Getty Images, 23; Mark Duncan/AP Images, 28; Gene J. Puskar/AP Images, 30; Tony Dejak/AP Images, 33; Scott Boehm/AP Images, 35; Winslow Townson/AP Images, 38; David Richard/AP Images, 41

Editor: Patrick Donnelly
Series Designer: Craig Hinton

Library of Congress Control Number: 2018964509

Publisher's Cataloging-in-Publication Data

Names: Hunter, Tony, author.
Title: Cleveland Browns / by Tony Hunter.
Description: Minneapolis, Minnesota : Abdo Publishing, 2020 | Series: Inside the NFL | Includes online resources and index.
Identifiers: ISBN 9781532118432 (lib. bdg.) | ISBN 9781532172618 (ebook)
Subjects: LCSH: Cleveland Browns (Football team : 1999-)--Juvenile literature. | National Football League--Juvenile literature. | Football teams--Juvenile literature. | American football--Juvenile literature.
Classification: DDC 796.33264--dc23

TABLE OF CONTENTS

MAJOR UPSET

Nobody believed that the Cleveland Browns would defeat the mighty Baltimore Colts in the 1964 National Football League (NFL) Championship Game. That is, nobody but the Cleveland Browns.

The Colts were downright scary. They posted a 12–2 record that year and had lost only once since Week 1. Baltimore's offense was led by Johnny Unitas, the finest quarterback in the NFL. The team's defense had given up seven points or fewer in five separate games.

The Browns, on the other hand? They had played well in the regular season. But they were far from dominant. They had lost three games and tied another. Their defense had given up the most yards in the NFL. It's no wonder they were given little chance to beat the Colts.

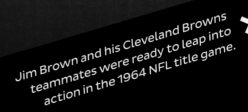

Jim Brown and his Cleveland Browns teammates were ready to leap into action in the 1964 NFL title game.

WHOOPS!

Sports Illustrated certainly goofed as the 1964 NFL title game approached. Its editors were so certain of the outcome that they had photos of Baltimore coach Don Shula and quarterback Johnny Unitas placed on the cover before the game was even played. When the Browns upset the Colts, the magazine's editors had to scramble to fix their mistake. They redid the cover with a picture of Cleveland quarterback Frank Ryan.

The showdown took place in Cleveland two days after Christmas. A bitterly cold wind whipped around Municipal Stadium. Both offenses struggled early, and the score at halftime was still 0–0. The Browns were encouraged.

After all, their defense had shut out Unitas and the powerful Colts for one half. If they could jump-start their own passing attack and sensational running back Jim Brown, they could win the championship.

That is exactly what happened. The combination of quarterback Frank Ryan and wide receiver Gary Collins got rolling. After a Lou Groza field goal opened the scoring, Ryan and Collins hooked up on touchdown strikes of 18 and 42 yards to give the Browns a 17–0 lead.

The Browns had the momentum, and they ran away with it. A 51-yard Ryan-to-Collins scoring pass made it 27–0. Meanwhile, Brown rushed for 114 yards, and what had been a mediocre defense that allowed the highest completion

Cleveland wide receiver Gary Collins, *left*, catches a touchdown pass against the Green Bay Packers.

percentage in the NFL that season limited Unitas to 95 passing yards and even intercepted two of his throws.

"We had a collective attitude that nobody was going to beat us," offensive guard Jim Houston said. "That is a remarkable feeling."

GREATEST PLAYER EVER

The debate has raged for decades: Who is the best player in NFL history? A small number of stars are generally mentioned. And Pro Football Hall of Fame running back Jim Brown is almost always in the mix.

Drafted by the Browns out of Syracuse University in 1957, Brown dominated the NFL from the start. He led the league in rushing yards as a rookie, the first of Brown's eight rushing titles in his nine NFL seasons.

In 1963 Brown ran for an NFL-record 1,863 yards, a mark that stood for a decade. His single-season average of 6.4 yards per attempt that year was the best in league history for any back with at least 200 carries. Kansas City Chiefs tailback Jamaal Charles matched the record in 2010. Some of Brown's other records have since been broken. It's possible that Brown would still hold many of them had he not retired at age 29 to pursue an acting career.

And when the final seconds ticked off the clock in Cleveland's 27–0 victory, many in the crowd of almost 80,000 rushed onto the Municipal Stadium field and tore down the goalposts to celebrate the championship.

They had no way of knowing that more than 50 years later, Browns fans would still be waiting to celebrate another title.

✕ Browns quarterback Frank Ryan gives a salute after Cleveland's 27–0 win over Baltimore in the 1964 NFL Championship Game.

CHAPTER 2

FAST START

The Browns' upset win over the Colts in the 1964 NFL Championship Game excited fans in Cleveland. But they were used to celebrating titles. The Browns were founding members of the All-America Football Conference (AAFC). The league existed for four seasons, from 1946 through 1949. The Browns won the title each year. Their record was 52–4–3 during that time.

It is well known that the 1972 Miami Dolphins were the first team to have ever completed an NFL championship season undefeated. The Dolphins went 14–0 in the regular season. Then they won three playoff games, including Super Bowl VII, to finish 17–0. But fewer are aware that the Browns accomplished a similar feat in the AAFC in 1948. They won all 14 regular-season games and capped off their

Quarterback Otto Graham, left, and coach Paul Brown led a successful transition from the AAFC to the NFL.

✗ Mac Speedie carries the ball during Cleveland's NFL debut against the Philadelphia Eagles on September 16, 1950.

incredible run by clobbering the Buffalo Bills 49–7 in the league championship game.

However, when the AAFC folded and the Browns were accepted into the NFL, the skeptics had a field day. They claimed that the team from Cleveland would be destroyed by

BROWN'S BROWNS

The history of the Cleveland Browns begins with Paul Brown. Co-owner Arthur McBride named the team after its first head coach, who was already famous in Ohio as a high school and college coach. Brown styled the team's uniforms and affixed no logo to the orange helmets. The Browns remain the only team in the NFL with a plain helmet. He pioneered the use of playbooks. This resulted in more complex offenses and defenses. It also made it harder for other teams to prepare for games against the Browns. He began the practice of studying footage of opponents to construct a better game plan for his team. He also popularized the use of full-time assistant coaches and opened his roster to black players long before other professional teams did. Owner Art Modell created plenty of protest when he fired Brown as coach after the 1962 season. Brown entered the Pro Football Hall of Fame in 1967. In 1968, he returned to the sideline as owner, general manager, and coach of the expansion Cincinnati Bengals.

the established clubs from a superior league. The Browns got an early test, playing the defending champion Philadelphia Eagles in the first game of the 1950 season.

While the Browns were dominating the AAFC, George Preston Marshall, owner of the NFL's Washington Redskins, was asked what he thought about the AAFC. "The worst team in our league could beat the best team in theirs," he said. NFL fans buzzed with anticipation. They could not wait to hear that the upstart Browns had been drubbed by the powerful Eagles.

BRILLIANT BACKS

The Browns were long known for their superb running backs. The first was a 232-pound bruiser named Marion Motley. Motley was among the top four rushers in the AAFC during all four years of its existence, and he led the league in 1948. By the time the Browns were absorbed into the NFL, he was 30 years old and had two failing knees. But he just picked up where he left off, winning the NFL rushing title in 1950.

In the early 1960s, though, tragedy hit the Browns at the running back spot. In 1961, they acquired Heisman Trophy winner Ernie Davis. He had been drafted that year by Washington and then traded to Cleveland. Davis had followed in Jim Brown's footsteps at the University of Syracuse, and they might have been unstoppable together in Cleveland. But Davis never played a game in the NFL. He was diagnosed with leukemia and died in the summer of 1962.

Browns coach Paul Brown never joined the war of words. He bided his time. And on September 16, 1950, his team silenced the critics.

The Browns didn't just win. They thrashed the stunned Eagles 35–10. Hall of Fame quarterback Otto Graham threw for 346 yards and three touchdowns—one to halfback Dub Jones and one each to wide receivers Dante Lavelli and Mac Speedie.

Brown did not reply to those who claimed his team played inferior football. Instead, he placed newspaper clippings filled

Cleveland's star running back Marion Motley was one of the first black players in professional football.

with their quotes on the team's bulletin board. Those clippings inspired his team to prove the critics wrong.

"For four years, Coach Brown never said a word; he just kept putting that stuff on the bulletin board," Graham said.

"THE TOE"

Some Browns fans remember Lou "The Toe" Groza only as a chubby placekicker. True, he booted many important field goals near the end of his career. But Groza, who wore his familiar number 76 uniform for most of his career, was among the finest offensive linemen in the game from 1948 to 1959. He even earned the NFL Player of the Year award in 1954. Through 2018, he still held the NFL record with five seasons leading the league in field goals. When he left the sport in 1968, he had scored 1,608 points—more than any player in NFL history. Fittingly, the address of the Browns' headquarters is 76 Lou Groza Boulevard.

"We were so fired up; we would have played [the Eagles] anywhere, anytime, for a keg of beer or a chocolate milkshake. It didn't matter."

The Browns steamrolled through the NFL just as they did the AAFC. Their opponents no longer took Graham's bunch lightly.

Lou Groza was the hero in the 1950 title game. He kicked a field goal with 28 seconds left to give the Browns a 30–28 win over the Los Angeles Rams. The Browns then embarked on a period of dominance never before seen in the NFL. They reached the championship game in six consecutive seasons and won three crowns.

Perhaps the most satisfying victory came in 1954. The Browns had lost to the Detroit Lions in the 1952 and 1953 NFL title games. But they got their revenge in 1954. The championship was all but decided when they sprinted to a 35–10 halftime lead. The Browns cruised to a 56–10 thumping of the Lions. Graham led the way, passing for three touchdowns and running for three more.

The game's biggest stars, however, performed for Cleveland's defense. They set an NFL Championship Game record by intercepting six passes against Detroit Hall of Fame quarterback Bobby Layne. The Browns added three fumble recoveries for an incredible nine turnovers on the day.

"I saw it, but still hardly can believe it," Lions coach Buddy Parker said after the game. "It has me dazed."

Graham went out with a bang the next year. He retired after leading the Browns to yet another title. This one was clinched with a 38–14 victory over the Rams in the NFL Championship Game.

Despite Graham's departure, the Browns continued to win. They played for the title in 1957 and won it again in 1964. They eventually declined. But not before they flirted with Super Bowl berths twice in the late 1960s.

CHAPTER 3

END OF GREATNESS

Browns fans began waiting for another NFL title after the championship win in 1964. As of 2019, they were still waiting. The team, however, did not collapse after 1964. The Browns remained one of the NFL's best teams through 1972. They lost the NFL Championship Game to the powerful Green Bay Packers in 1965. Then their star running back, Jim Brown, shocked the world by retiring in the prime of his career.

The Browns then unveiled their third Hall of Fame running back in a row. Leroy Kelly picked up where Marion Motley and Brown left off. Kelly helped Cleveland make its way into the playoffs five times in a six-year span ending in 1972. He led the team to upset victories over the Dallas Cowboys in the first rounds of the 1968 and 1969 playoffs.

Cleveland running back Jim Brown looks on during a game in 1965. Brown, still in his prime, retired after the season.

THE OLD SWITCHEROO

The NFL's 1970 merger with the AFL affected the Browns greatly. The new arrangement divided the NFL into the American Football Conference (AFC) and National Football Conference (NFC). But three NFL teams had to agree to join the AFC to give each conference the same number of teams. Browns owner Art Modell asked for his team to be one of them. The Browns have played in the AFC ever since.

The Browns were on the verge of qualifying for the Super Bowl. The game had debuted after the 1966 season. It pitted the NFL champion against the winner of the upstart American Football League (AFL). But the Browns lost NFL title games against the Baltimore Colts in 1968 and the Minnesota Vikings in 1969 by a combined score of 61–7.

Owner Art Modell decided to make a bold move—but it resulted in disaster. After the 1969 season, he traded future Hall of Fame wide receiver Paul Warfield for the rights to move up to the third spot in the draft, where the club selected Purdue quarterback Mike Phipps. Phipps failed miserably. So did the Browns.

Phipps got off to a promising start. He led the Browns to the playoffs and a near upset of unbeaten Miami in 1972. But two years later, the Browns suffered through the second losing season in their history.

✕ Browns running back Leroy Kelly looks for room to run against the Vikings in the NFL Championship Game.

Cleveland then lost its first nine games in 1975. The Browns recovered during the rest of the decade to play decent football. Then quarterback Brian Sipe blossomed in Cleveland, giving Browns fans hope for a return to greatness. In 1980 Sipe led the Browns on perhaps their most magical run. He guided the team to a series of heart-stopping comeback victories. The thrilling games the young Browns played nearly every Sunday earned them the nickname "the Kardiac Kids." And the fans could hardly contain their joy when their team earned a playoff spot by winning its division.

The windchill factor was minus 36 degrees Fahrenheit (minus 38°C) on January 4, 1981. Nearly 80,000 fans bundled up to watch their beloved Browns play the Oakland Raiders.

The Browns trailed 14–12 with just a few minutes remaining. But Sipe and running back Mike Pruitt led a charge downfield. They reached Oakland's 13-yard line. Browns coach Sam Rutigliano had to make a decision. Should he send out kicker Don Cockroft to attempt to win the game with a field goal? It would be only 30 yards. But the wind was howling, the snow was falling, and Cockroft had been struggling.

Rutigliano was a gambler. He decided that he would try for a touchdown. He called for a play known as "Red Right 88"—words that still sting Browns fans everywhere. Sipe fired a pass into the end zone to sure-handed tight end Ozzie Newsome. But it was intercepted by the Raiders' Mike Davis. The game was lost.

"We've lived and died with the pass all year long," Newsome said in the gloomy Browns locker room. "This time we died."

✕ Oakland's Mike Davis intercepts a pass intended for Cleveland's Ozzie Newsome on the "Red Right 88" play on January 4, 1981.

The Browns were dead for a while. They did not recover until another quarterback hero arrived in 1985. And this one came right from their own backyard.

CHAPTER 4

SO CLOSE, YET SO FAR

Bernie Kosar looked funny tossing a football. His sidearm delivery was slow and awkward. Yet he found success because of his intelligence and accuracy.

When Kosar was growing up in nearby Youngstown, Ohio, he was a big Browns fan. After a stellar career at the University of Miami in Florida, he was taken by his hometown team in the 1985 supplemental draft. That selection launched a period of excellence for the Browns. They qualified for the playoffs in each of the next five years.

The Browns had developed a fine team. Kosar had plenty of weapons available, including running backs Earnest Byner and Kevin Mack and tight end Ozzie Newsome. The defense featured a strong secondary led by cornerbacks

Cleveland quarterback Bernie Kosar threw the ball in an unusual way, but he was very successful.

Hanford Dixon and Frank Minnifield. Clay Matthews was among the top linebackers in the league.

The Browns reached the AFC title game after the 1986, 1987, and 1989 seasons. But they lost all three to the Denver Broncos. The most frustrating defeat was the first one. Playing in front of their passionate fans, the Browns forged ahead 20–13 on a touchdown pass from Kosar to Brian Brennan with less than six minutes remaining.

Those remaining minutes were all that stood between the Browns and their first Super Bowl berth. But Denver quarterback John Elway engineered a 98-yard touchdown drive that tied the score, and the Browns lost 23–20 in overtime.

After the game, the Browns were stunned. "It's hard to believe that it happened," Kosar said, while defensive lineman Bob Golic added, "It's the lowest thing that's ever happened to me, as far back as I can remember."

✕ The Browns' Chris Rockins (37) and Ray Ellis tackle Denver's Gerald Willhite in the AFC title game in January 1987.

The Browns lost another heartbreaker in the AFC title game a year later, this time in Denver. They were on their way to a potential game-tying touchdown when Byner fumbled on the Broncos' 3-yard line to seal Denver's victory. Though the Browns reached the doorstep of a Super Bowl again in 1989, they have never truly recovered.

 A fan cheers in the Dawg Pound section at Cleveland's Municipal Stadium during a playoff game after the 1987 season.

When the Browns released Kosar in 1993, fans were outraged—despite the fact that the team was in the midst of its fourth consecutive losing season. Kosar went on to sign with Dallas. He was replaced at quarterback by Vinny Testaverde, who helped the Browns reach the playoffs in 1994.

By that time, however, owner Art Modell was showing signs of discontent. He was angry that the city of Cleveland had agreed to build a new baseball stadium for the Indians and a basketball arena for the Cavaliers. Modell waited in vain for a new football stadium for his Browns. And few could have predicted what he did in 1995.

On November 6, Modell held a press conference. He announced that he had not only decided to move the Browns,

"THE DAWGS"

In the summer of 1985, Browns cornerback Hanford Dixon coined a nickname for the team's defense that is still used today.

"We didn't have a great defensive line, and I was just thinking of a way to get those guys going," he explained. "I started barking at them. The fans . . . were so close to the [practice] fields, they'd hear me and [fellow cornerback Frank Minnifield] barking, and they'd bark back."

Dixon started calling the Cleveland defense "the Dawgs." He even placed a banner in the bleachers at Municipal Stadium that proclaimed it "the Dawg Pound."

Dixon and Minnifield made the new nickname popular by barking during radio and television interviews. They also backed up their bravado on the field. During the second half of the 1980s, no cornerback combination in the NFL proved more effective in covering receivers.

ART - YOU
BROKE
CLEVELAND'S

The Browns' fans left no question about how they felt when owner Art Modell announced his intention to move the team.

but that the deal was already done. He and the Browns were leaving for Baltimore after the season.

Fans were angry. The city of Cleveland was angry. The city even tried suing Modell, saying he was required to fulfill his stadium lease. But Modell would not budge.

The Browns played out the rest of the season in Cleveland. They were 4–5 when the move was announced. Then the team took a nosedive and finished 5–11. The last game the Browns won was also their last home game. Players waved goodbye after beating the Cincinnati Bengals. Some fans cried. It was an emotional scene for both the team and its fans.

TITLE IN BALTIMORE

When the Browns moved to Baltimore after the 1995 season, they became known as the Baltimore Ravens. The Ravens inherited the Browns' players but were considered a new team. Led by linebacker Ray Lewis, drafted in 1996, Baltimore improved quickly. The improvement was so swift that the 2000 Ravens reached the Super Bowl and won it, 34–7 over the New York Giants.

After the season, the city, Modell, and the NFL made a compromise. The team was going to move. But the Browns' name, colors, history, and everything else associated with the team would stay. Cleveland would get a new team in three years, and it would continue the Browns history.

The existing Browns instead became the Baltimore Ravens. Though the Cleveland fans were getting a new team, it was tough for fans to watch their favorite players wear strange new uniforms in a different city.

CHAPTER 5

STRUGGLES CONTINUE

The Browns returned in 1999. Fans were thrilled to have their team back. But those who expected the glory days to return were in for a bumpy ride.

A series of poor decisions, including a number of bad draft selections, kept Cleveland near the bottom of the standings almost every season through 2017. The Browns failed to achieve consistency during that time, bringing in new coaches and overhauling the team every few years.

From 1999 through 2017, the Browns compiled a lowly record of 88–216. They reached the postseason just once in that span, losing in the first round of the 2002 AFC playoffs. They managed just two winning records in 19 seasons.

The Browns returned to the NFL with an expansion team in 1999.

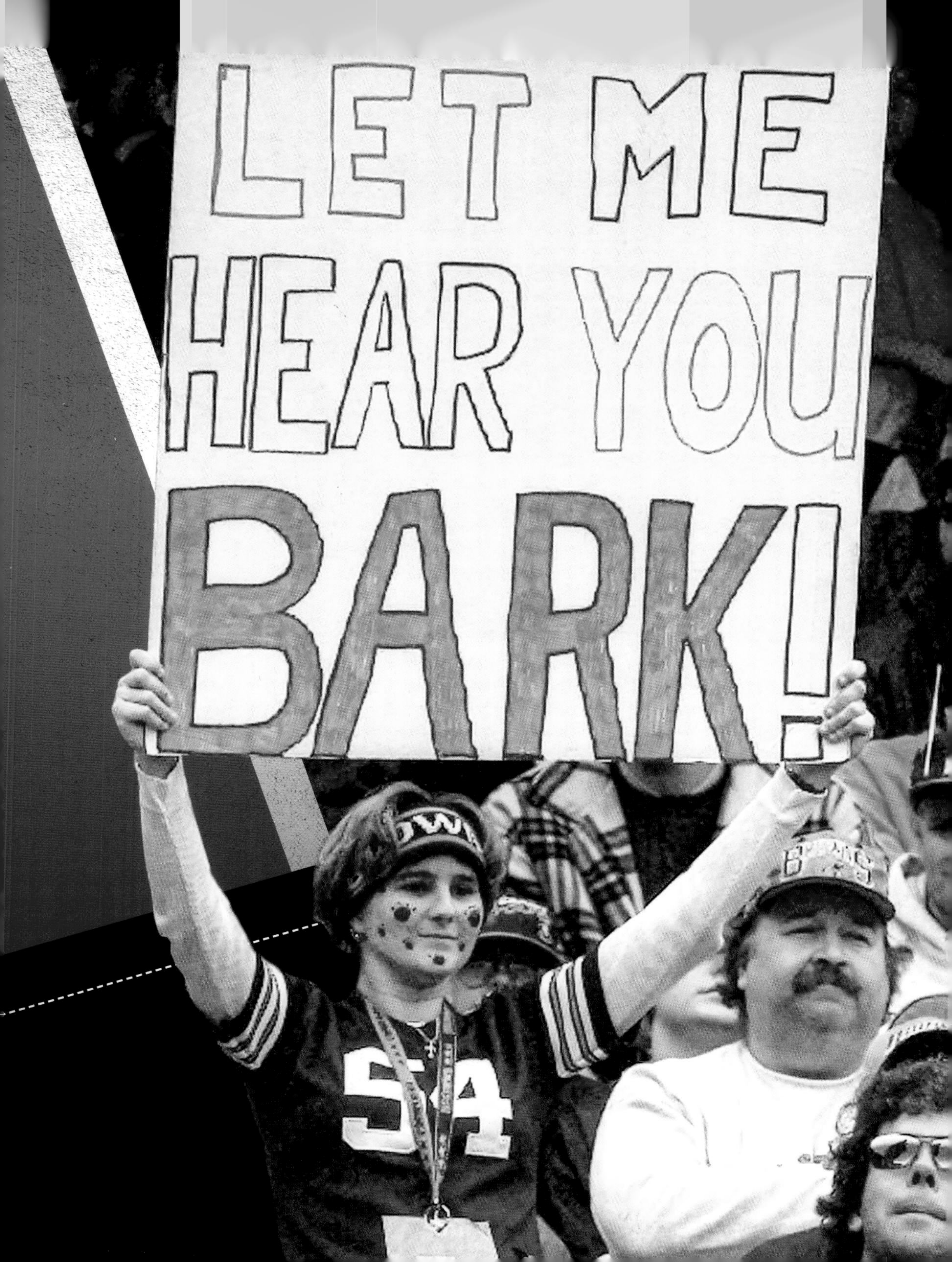
LET ME
HEAR YOU
BARK!
54

MORE FRUSTRATION

It appeared that the Browns were going to win in their first playoff game since their return to town. On January 5, 2003, they led the host Pittsburgh Steelers 33–21 in the fourth quarter. Two touchdown passes from Kelly Holcomb to Dennis Northcutt helped Cleveland take that lead. Holcomb had a big game filling in for the injured Tim Couch, going 26-for-43 for 429 yards and three touchdowns. But Browns fans had grown accustomed to disappointment, and they were to be disappointed again. The Steelers scored two late touchdowns to win 36–33. Pittsburgh, Cleveland's biggest rival, enjoyed a particularly dominant stretch in the series, winning 18 of 19 meetings between the two teams until falling to the Browns late in the 2009 season. Cleveland then won just two of its next 18 games against the Steelers.

After head coach Chris Palmer was ineffective in two seasons, the team hired Butch Davis for 2001. The Browns did show some signs of life with a 2002 playoff appearance. Quarterback Tim Couch, the first overall pick in the 1999 NFL Draft, started 14 games as the Browns went 9–7. But Couch never turned into the franchise quarterback the Browns had hoped. He was released after the 2003 season and never played in the NFL again.

In 2005 the Browns made another coaching change and hired former Patriots defensive coordinator Romeo Crennel.

✖ Quarterback Derek Anderson led the Browns to 10 wins in 2007.

He guided Cleveland to a surprising 10-win season in 2007, though tiebreakers kept them out of the playoffs. The Browns had one of the league's top offenses, led by running back Jamal Lewis. Lewis rushed for 1,304 yards. They also had two top receivers in Kellen Winslow and Braylon Edwards. Each had more than 1,000 yards receiving.

NO ORDINARY JOE

It is unusual that a team's franchise player is an offensive lineman. But for the Cleveland Browns of the 2000s, that's exactly what Joe Thomas was. He was a steady presence in the middle of a lot of losing.

The Browns made one of the few excellent draft picks of their modern era when they selected Thomas with the third pick of the 2007 draft. Thomas became a starter on the offensive line right away. And he just kept on starting.

Not only did Thomas not miss a game in his first 10 seasons, he never missed a snap. His streak of 10,363 snaps in a row is believed to be an NFL record. His streak came to an end when he was injured on October 22, 2017, against the Tennessee Titans. He ended up missing the rest of the season.

After 11 seasons and 10 Pro Bowl appearances, Thomas decided to retire after 2017. He was inducted into the Browns Ring of Honor during the 2018 season.

Another coaching change in 2009 brought in Eric Mangini, another former New England assistant who had been head coach of the New York Jets as well. In his first year, the Browns won their last four games. Team owner Randy Lerner added to the optimism by luring Mike Holmgren to become team president. Holmgren had been to the Super Bowl three times as a head coach of the Green Bay Packers and the Seattle Seahawks. He took over the hiring of coaches and players.

But once again, the Browns did not build on that promise. Mangini lasted just one more season as the Browns went 5–11. In the next six years, the Browns made four more coaching changes, but they kept spinning their wheels. Pat Shurmur went 9–23 in two seasons. Rob Chudzinski went 4–12 in his one season as head coach. Mike Pettine went 10–22.

In 2016 the Browns hired Hue Jackson. He was a longtime NFL assistant coach and had been a successful offensive coordinator. The Browns hoped to finally have some stability in coaching.

The players liked Jackson. But in his first year, the Browns were dreadful. They lost their first 14 games and looked like a safe bet to join the 2008 Detroit Lions as the only teams to go 0–16 in a season. But on Christmas Eve against the San Diego Chargers, a late defensive stand and a missed field goal at the gun gave the

CLOSE CALL

Browns fans will always ask, "What if?" about the 2007 Browns. Despite a top-10 offense and 10 wins, the team still managed to miss the playoffs. They lost twice to the Steelers, so Pittsburgh—which had the same record as Cleveland—won the AFC North on that tiebreaker. The Tennessee Titans also went 10–6, and they had a better record against common opponents—teams the Titans and Browns both had played that year. So the Browns missed out on a wild-card spot despite posting their best record since 1994.

Browns a 20–17 victory. They lost their final game to go 1–15, the worst record in team history. But Jackson stayed confident. He made a promise that Cleveland would not be that bad again. If they were, he said he would jump in Lake Erie.

In 2017 the Browns did not go 1–15 again. They went 0–16. True to his word, Jackson did jump in the frigid lake the following January. Not only did the Browns match the Lions' infamous mark. Cleveland's two-year record of 1–31 was the worst in NFL history. Forget about making the playoffs. The team was just trying to win a game.

One reason for optimism before 2018 came in the NFL Draft. The Browns had tried many quarterbacks. But in taking Heisman Trophy winner Baker Mayfield first overall, they hoped they finally made the right choice. Mayfield did not start the season. But fans were excited for him to take over.

The Browns made progress in Week 1 of the 2018 season. They did not lose. They tied the rival Pittsburgh Steelers 21–21. The next week, the New Orleans Saints kicked a field goal in the final minute to beat the Browns 21–18, extending the winless streak.

Cleveland next played the New York Jets on national television. Starting quarterback Tyrod Taylor got hurt with the Browns down 14–0 in the first half. Mayfield got his chance. He led Cleveland to a field goal before the half.

In the second half, Mayfield was almost perfect. He led the Browns on three more scoring drives to beat the Jets 21–17.

In all, Mayfield went 17-for-23 for 201 yards. He even caught a pass for a two-point conversion that tied the game. It was the first Browns win in 20 games, a span of 635 days.

Unfortunately for Jackson, Mayfield's play didn't save his job. He was fired after a 2–5–1 start in 2018. Mayfield continued to play well, finishing his rookie season with 27 touchdown passes in 13 starts as the team finished 7–8–1. And even though he was just a rookie, Mayfield's performance stirred the imagination of Browns fans.

After the season, the team hired former offensive coordinator Freddie Kitchens as its new head coach and added star wide receiver Odell Beckham Jr. in a trade with the New York Giants. After the pain of losing their team to Baltimore, and the pain of losing on the field, the new quarterback, wide receiver, and head coach provided the most hope Browns fans have had in years.

JOHNNY FOOTBALL

Baker Mayfield is not the first Heisman Trophy–winning quarterback the Browns have deemed a franchise savior. Johnny Manziel was Cleveland's top draft choice in 2014. Manziel had been a game-changing quarterback at Texas A&M. But he ran into trouble both on and off the field in the NFL. After putting up with his personal issues for two years, the Browns released him following the 2015 season.

✕ Baker Mayfield's strong play early in the 2018 season had Browns fans looking forward to the future.

TIMELINE

The Browns are founded as an AAFC franchise by owner Arthur McBride. Paul Brown is the first coach and runs the organization.

1944

The host Browns win the first AAFC title on December 22 by defeating the New York Yankees 14–9.

1946

The Browns earn a clean sweep of AAFC championships by winning their fourth straight before the league folds. Cleveland defeats the visiting San Francisco 49ers 21–7 on December 11.

1949

The Browns crush the Philadelphia Eagles 35–10 in their first NFL game and go on to win the NFL crown in their first year in the league.

1950

After losing two straight years to Detroit in the NFL title game, the host Browns rout the Lions 56–10 for the championship on December 26.

1954

The Browns capture their second NFL title in a row with a 38–14 road victory over the Rams on December 26. It was Graham's last game, as he retires after the season.

1955

The Browns draft running back Jim Brown, who blossoms into one of the greatest players in NFL history.

1957

The Browns win their last title on December 27, defeating the heavily favored Baltimore Colts 27–0 in Cleveland.

1964

The Browns defeat the Dallas Cowboys to reach the NFL Championship Game. But they fall 34–0 to the visiting Colts on December 29 with a Super Bowl berth on the line.

1968

The Browns again beat the Cowboys in the first round of the playoffs, but this time they lose to the host Minnesota Vikings 27–7 in the NFL title game on January 4.

1970

The "Kardiac Kids" lose a heartbreaking first-round playoff game 14–12 to the visiting Oakland Raiders on January 4.

The Browns compile the best record in the AFC but lose 23–20 in overtime to the visiting Denver Broncos with a Super Bowl berth on the line on January 11.

Earnest Byner's fumble dooms the Browns in yet another AFC title game defeat against the Broncos, this time in Denver on January 17.

Owner Art Modell announces on November 6 that he is moving the Browns to Baltimore.

The Browns play their first game in four years in Cleveland. They fall 43–0 to the Pittsburgh Steelers on September 12.

1981

1987

1988

1995

1999

The Browns qualify for the playoffs for the first time since returning to Cleveland. They lose 36–33 to host Pittsburgh on January 5.

A missed field goal on the game's last play gives the Browns a 20–17 victory over San Diego on December 24. It's Cleveland's only win of the season.

The Browns become the second NFL team to go 0–16. Their two-year record of 1–31 is the worst in league history.

The Browns draft Heisman Trophy winner Baker Mayfield first overall. He rallies the team to its first win in two seasons in Week 3.

The Browns finish the season 7–8–1, their best record since 2007.

2003

2016

2017

2018

2018

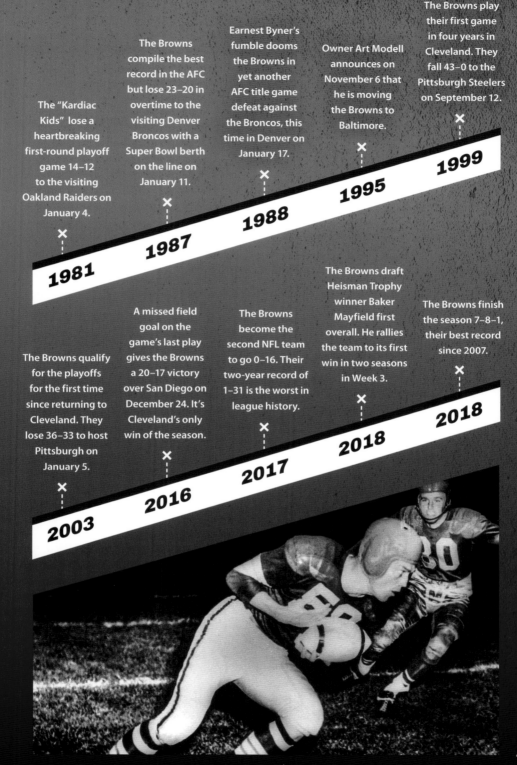

QUICK STATS

FRANCHISE HISTORY

1946–49 (AAFC)
1950–96 (NFL)
1999– (NFL)

SUPER BOWLS

None

AAFC CHAMPIONSHIP GAMES *(1946–49, wins in bold)*

1946, **1947**, **1948**, **1949**

NFL CHAMPIONSHIP GAMES *(1950–69, wins in bold)*

1950, 1951, 1952, 1953, **1954**, **1955**, 1957, **1964**, 1965, 1968, 1969

AFC CHAMPIONSHIP GAMES *(since 1970 AFL-NFL merger)*

1986, 1987, 1989

DIVISION CHAMPIONSHIPS *(since 1970 AFL-NFL merger)*

1971, 1980, 1985, 1986, 1987, 1989

KEY COACHES

Paul Brown (1946–62): 158–48–8, 9–5 (playoffs)
Blanton Collier (1963–70): 76–34–2, 3–4 (playoffs)

KEY PLAYERS *(position, seasons with team)*

Jim Brown (RB, 1957–65)
Len Ford (DE, 1950–57)
Frank Gatski (C, 1946–56)
Otto Graham (QB, 1946–55)
Lou Groza (OT/K, 1946–59, 1961–67)
Leroy Kelly (RB, 1964–73)
Bernie Kosar (QB, 1985–93)
Dante Lavelli (WR, 1946–56)
Clay Matthews (LB, 1978–93)
Marion Motley (RB, 1946–53)
Ozzie Newsome (TE, 1978–90)
Brian Sipe (QB, 1974–83)
Joe Thomas (OT, 2007–17)
Paul Warfield (WR, 1964–69, 1976–77)

HOME FIELDS

FirstEnergy Stadium (1999–)
Formerly known as Cleveland Browns Stadium
Cleveland Municipal Stadium (1946–95)

* All statistics through 2018 season

QUOTES AND ANECDOTES

Who was the last Browns player to win the NFL Most Valuable Player Award? It was quarterback Brian Sipe, who captured it for leading the team to the playoffs in 1980.

The Browns once had a defensive lineman named Cleveland Crosby. One day he showed up to a meeting wearing a T-shirt bearing the name of the Browns' hated rivals, the Pittsburgh Steelers. Coach Sam Rutigliano forced Crosby to remove the shirt and sit in the meeting bare-chested.

One of the smallest players in Browns history was wide receiver and kick returner Gerald "Ice Cube" McNeil. When McNeil arrived for his first day of practice in 1986, he asked team publicist Dino Lucarelli for tickets for his family and friends.

"I'm sorry," Lucarelli replied. "I can only get tickets for players."

"I am a player," McNeil said. "I'm Gerald McNeil."

Lucarelli later confessed that he thought McNeil was a ball boy. After all, McNeil was just 5-foot-7 and weighed 140 pounds.

Baker Mayfield provided a unique hangout for Browns quarterbacks during the team's 2018 training camp. The rookie rented an RV and called it a "top-secret clubhouse" that was off-limits to everyone but the team's signal-callers. It was a quiet place where they could bond and talk about quarterback matters.

GLOSSARY

comeback
When a team losing a game rallies to tie the score or take the lead.

franchise
A sports organization, including the top-level team and all minor league affiliates.

Heisman Trophy
The award given yearly to the best player in college football.

legendary
A player who is generally regarded as one of the best to ever play.

momentum
The sense that a team is playing well and will be difficult to stop.

Pro Bowl
The NFL's all-star game, in which the best players in the league compete.

retire
To end one's career.

rookie
A professional athlete in his or her first year of competition.

secondary
The defensive players—cornerbacks and safeties—who start the play farthest away from the line.

MORE INFORMATION

BOOKS

Cohn, Nate. *Cleveland Browns*. New York: AV2 by Weigl, 2018.

Scheff, Matt. *Best NFL Running Backs of All Time.* Minneapolis, MN: Abdo Publishing, 2013.

Tustison, Matt. *Cleveland Browns*. Minneapolis, MN: Abdo Publishing, 2017.

ONLINE RESOURCES

To learn more about the Cleveland Browns, visit **abdobooklinks.com** or scan this QR code. These links are routinely monitored and updated to provide the most current information available.

PLACE TO VISIT

FirstEnergy Stadium
100 Alfred Lerner Way
Cleveland, OH 44114
440–891–5001
firstenergystadium.com

In addition to being the Browns' home field, FirstEnergy Stadium has hosted other sporting events such as international soccer. It also hosts major concerts.

INDEX

ABOUT THE AUTHOR

Tony Hunter is a writer from Castle Rock, Colorado. This is his first children's book series. He lives with his daughter and his trusty Rottweiler, Dan.